The Gypsy Moth In America

Leland Ossian Howard

In the interest of creating a more extensive selection of rare historical book reprints, we have chosen to reproduce this title even though it may possibly have occasional imperfections such as missing and blurred pages, missing text, poor pictures, markings, dark backgrounds and other reproduction issues beyond our control. Because this work is culturally important, we have made it available as a part of our commitment to protecting, preserving and promoting the world's literature. Thank you for your understanding.

BULLETIN No. 11—NEW SERIES.

U. S. DEPARTMENT OF AGRICULTURE.

DIVISION OF ENTOMOLOGY.

THE

GIPSY MOTH IN AMERICA:

A Summary Account of the Introduction and Spread of Porthetria
dispar in Massachusetts and of the Efforts Made by
the State to Repress and Exterminate it.

BY

L. O. HOWARD,

ENTOMOLOGIST.

WASHINGTON:
GOVERNMENT PRINTING OFFICE.
1897.

LETTER OF TRANSMITTAL.

U. S. DEPARTMENT OF AGRICULTURE,
DIVISION OF ENTOMOLOGY,
Washington, D. C., November 30, 1897.

SIR: I have the honor to submit for publication an account of the Gipsy Moth (*Porthetria dispar*) in Massachusetts and the efforts which the State has been making to exterminate it. This report has been prepared in accordance with a provision made in the appropriation bill for this Department for the fiscal year ending June 30, 1898. I recommend it for publication as Bulletin No. 11, new series, of this division.

Respectfully,

L. O. HOWARD,
Entomologist.

Hon. JAMES WILSON,
Secretary of Agriculture.

CONTENTS.

	Page
Introduction: Reasons for this publication	5
The Gipsy Moth in Europe	6
Life history of the insect	6
Appearance of the Gipsy Moth in America	7
A review of the State legislation	9
Methods used by the State authorities	14
Opposition to the State work	22
The investigation of the work by the writer during 1897	23
Present condition of the infested territory	24
Conclusions	37

ILLUSTRATIONS.

FIG. 1. Female Gipsy Moth... 5
  2. Male Gipsy Moth... 6
  3. Full-grown caterpillar of Gipsy Moth.. 7
  4. Pupa of Gipsy Moth.. 8
  5. Map showing the territory actually infested by the Gipsy Moth, as determined in 1891 by the State board of agriculture, and the areas supposed to be infested in 1889 and 1890......................... 10
  6. Map showing the region found infested in 1891, the colonies of the Gipsy Moth found since 1891 (but prior to 1896) outside that region, and the three principal centers of infestation and distribution in the woods.. 11
  7. Manner of applying burlap bands.. 18
  8. Map of the territory found infested in 1891, showing the relation of the distribution of the Gipsy Moth to population........................ 25

THE GIPSY MOTH IN AMERICA.

INTRODUCTION: REASONS FOR THIS PUBLICATION.

As almost everyone has learned through the publications of the State Board of Agriculture of Massachusetts and through the newspaper press, the Gipsy Moth of Europe was some years since accidentally introduced into the State of Massachusetts, flourished there to an alarming extent, and became as early as 1890 the subject of State investigation. Since 1890 large sums of money have been expended in the effort to exterminate the insect. All of the work has been done under State authority and with State funds. Outside entomologists of standing have occasionally been called in to advise the persons charged with the work, and in the winter of 1894-95 an unsuccessful attempt was made to secure aid from the National Government. In fact the United States Senate inserted an amendment to the appropriation bill for the Department of Agriculture allotting $40,000 for the purpose, but this amendment was not accepted by the House of Representatives and was eliminated in conference committee.

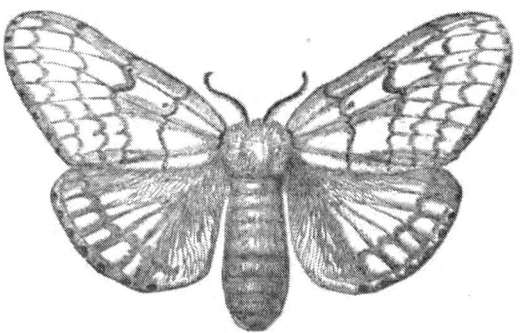

FIG. 1.—Female Gipsy Moth—natural size (from *Insect Life*).

In the session of Congress of 1896-97, however, a clause was added to the section making appropriations for entomological investigations under the Department, providing for "an investigation into the ravages of the Gipsy Moth." In conformity with this provision an investigation was duly undertaken in this division. This investigation has included a study of the extent and character of the ravages of this pest and of the remedial measures used by the State officials of Massachusetts, with the object in view of deciding upon the best course to pursue in the future. The insect is at present confined to eastern Massachusetts, and it is highly desirable not only to limit its spread, but also to exterminate it, if possible, in the territory already occupied.

THE GIPSY MOTH IN EUROPE.

Porthetria dispar is an old and well-known European insect. It occupies the whole of central and south Europe, flourishing in temperate regions and extending its range across temperate Asia to Japan. It is found as far south as Algeria, into which country it is supposed to have been introduced in comparatively recent years, but does not abound in England, and, in fact, is a very rare species in that country. In portions of France, Germany, and Russia it is considered to be an injurious insect of first-class importance. In the protected forests of these countries its ravages are occasionally excessive, while at frequent intervals the shade trees of the larger cities are completely stripped of their leaves. Few European insects have received more attention from the European foresters than this species. Books published as early as 1720 refer to its ravages. Judging from the European literature it does not appear in equal numbers every year, but will be excessively abundant in a certain region for two or three years in succession, and will then remain in comparative obscurity for several years, just as is the case with other noxious species, not only in Europe, but in this country as well.

FIG. 2.—Male Gipsy Moth—natural size (from *Insect Life*).

So far as can be learned no large scale remedies have been adopted in Europe. The intermittent character of the appearances of the insect in injurious numbers render remedial work necessary only at intervals. Aside from removing the egg clusters by hand, trapping the caterpillars with bands, and preventing their access to uninfested trees by means of sticky substances, no remedies worthy of detailed consideration have been adopted.

LIFE HISTORY OF THE INSECT.

All through its European range the Gipsy Moth has but one annual generation, and this statement applies equally well to Massachusetts. The eggs are about one-twentieth of an inch in diameter and are laid in clusters, each cluster containing from 400 to 500 eggs and varying in size from one-half to one and one-half inches in length and from one-third to one inch in width. Each cluster is covered with yellowish hairs from the body of the female moth, causing the cluster to resemble a bit of sponge in general appearance. These clusters are attached to the trunks of trees, to stones, to logs, and in all situations which can be reached by the females. The females have an especial propensity for crawling into crevices, thus frequently concealing their egg clusters from casual observation. The eggs are laid in the latter part of summer and the insect remains in the egg state for nine or ten months. The caterpillars hatch from the end of April until the middle of June, reach full growth in the course of about ten weeks, spin flimsy cocoons attached usually to the trunks of the trees, and within these cocoons transform to chrysalids, remaining in this stage from ten to thirteen days, and emerging as moths in late July or August.

The feeding of the caterpillars is done as a rule at night, except when they occur in very great numbers, and they are known to destroy the foliage of nearly every native and introduced plant of economic importance. During the first few weeks they remain most of the time on the leaves feeding on the under surface, but as they grow larger they crawl down the branches and the trunk toward the ground in the early mornings, and there seek protection under loosened bark or in cracks in the trunk or quite at the ground under leaves and rubbish, ascending again at nightfall to resume work upon the foliage. Upon this habit depends one of the best remedies, that of trapping the insects under bands, but also upon this habit depends possibly the main means of distribution of the species. The activity of the caterpillar is responsible in large measure for its spread.

The adult insect, or moth, although possessing what seems to be abundant wing surface in both sexes, flies readily only as a male. The female possesses such a heavy body that her aerial locomotion is limited to a few struggling flaps which result simply in lessening the force of her fall from a height. A female issuing from a cocoon high up on the trunk of a tree and falling from this cocoon, sometimes before laying her eggs and sometimes afterwards, is seldom able by the use of her wings to reach the ground at a greater distance than a few yards from the base of the tree.

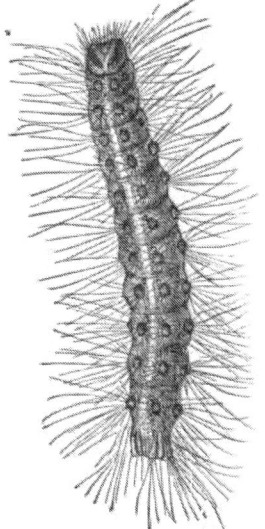

FIG. 3.—Full-grown caterpillar of Gipsy Moth—natural size (from *Insect Life*).

Many natural enemies of the Gipsy Moth are known in Europe. The writer has listed 28 species of hymenopterous parasites. Several dipterous species are also known to attack it, and many predatory insects as well as birds and other animals. Diseases of a bacterial or fungus nature frequently carry it off in large numbers, as is frequently the case with other caterpillars, both in Europe and in America.

APPEARANCE OF THE GIPSY MOTH IN AMERICA.

Through the efforts of the persons having the Massachusetts work in charge, it has been practically decided that this insect was first brought to the United States by Prof. L. Trouvelot, a naturalist and astronomer, in 1869. Professor Trouvelot was at that time connected with the astronomical observatory at Harvard University, and for his pleasure and interest was engaged in the study of wild silkworms with the idea that species of commercial value might be found, and that perhaps something might be done in the way of cross breeding allied species, thus producing not perhaps a better quality of silk than that of the silkworm of commerce, but a hardier insect, which would require less artificial attention and at the same time would be more resistant to disease. The whole experimentation, we believe, was suggested by the disastrous prevalence in the silkworm establishments of Europe of the pébrine disease, which some years later was controlled by virtue of Pasteur's discoveries.

In the course of this work Professor Trouvelot brought over from Europe living specimens of different silk-spinning caterpillars in different stages of existence. Among others he imported living egg clusters of the Gipsy Moth. He lived at No. 27 Myrtle street, Medford, and the insects escaped from his window into the adjoining garden. One story is that the eggs blew out of the window, and another that the caterpillars crawled out. He seems, however, to have done what he could to repair the damage, gave public notice of the escape of the species, and undoubtedly searched carefully for the missing eggs or larvæ. Unfortunately, the part of Medford in which he lived almost immediately adjoined an extensive wood lot, densely covered with underbrush, and in this jungle of vegetation the insect soon established itself. For many years, however, it was not noticed by the citizens of Medford, from which it is plain that it increased with extreme slowness. The principal reasons for this slow increase are supposed to be, first, that the insect was gradually accommodating itself to the severe climate; second, that the wood lot abounded with insectivorous birds, and, third, that almost annually it was burned over. That there was, however, a constant, though slow, increase is shown by the fact that after twelve or fifteen years the caterpillars began to be troublesome in the gardens of the residents of that portion of the town.

FIG. 4.—Pupa of Gipsy Moth—natural size (from *Insect Life*).

They fought it vigorously and undoubtedly retarded its increase by their individual activity, but by the summer of 1889 it had multiplied to such an extent as to become a notorious pest. In that summer its numbers were so enormous that the trees were completely stripped of their leaves, the crawling caterpillars covered the sidewalks, the trunks of the shade trees, the fences, and the sides of the houses, entering the houses, and getting into the food and into the beds. They were killed in countless numbers by the inhabitants, who swept them up into piles, poured kerosene over them, and set them on fire. Thousands upon thousands were crushed under the feet of pedestrians, and a pungent and filthy stench arose from their decaying bodies. The numbers were so great that in the still summer nights the sound of their feeding could plainly be heard, while the pattering of their excremental pellets on the ground sounded like a shower of rain. Valuable fruit and shade trees were killed in large numbers by their work and the value of real estate was very considerably reduced. So great was the nuisance that it was impossible, for example, to hang clothes upon the garden clothesline, as they would become covered with the caterpillars and stained with their excrement. Persons walking along the streets would become covered with caterpillars spinning down from the trees. To read the testimony of older inhabitants of the town, which has been collected and published by the Gipsy Moth committee, reminds one vividly of one of the biblical plagues of Egypt.

During all this time the Medford people had been under the impression that the insect which they were fighting in their gardens was a native species, and they knew it simply as "the caterpillar" or "army worm." There seem to have been no local entomologists, and no one appears to have taken the trouble to find out definitely what the insect might be. In June, 1889, Mr. John Stetson took a specimen to Hon. William R. Sessions, secretary of the State board of agriculture, for identification. The insect was new to Mr. Sessions, who advised Mr. Stetson to send it to the State Agricultural Experiment Station at Amherst. This was done, and in the absence of Professor Fernald in Europe, his wife, who is fortunately a learned entomologist herself, was able, after searching through the European books, to identify the insect as the larva of the well-known Gipsy Moth of Europe. The fact was immediately announced through the newspapers, and the writer, together with many others, gained his first knowledge of the occurrence through the "New England Farmer" of July 13, 1889.

A REVIEW OF THE STATE LEGISLATION.

The first combined effort to check the caterpillar was immediately undertaken. A town meeting was held on July 15, 1889, and the sum of $300 for the care of shade trees was appropriated, to be expended under the direction of the road commissioners. Men were employed to scrape off the egg clusters from shade trees, and much money and effort were expended by citizens on their own premises. In November an illustrated bulletin was issued, in an edition of 45,000 copies, by Professor Fernald, at the State Agricultural Experiment Station. It was mailed to taxpayers in Medford and vicinity, and was printed in full in one of the local papers of December 6. It was found during that winter that the insect was so numerous and so widely distributed that the town authorities could not successfully fight it and the legislature was

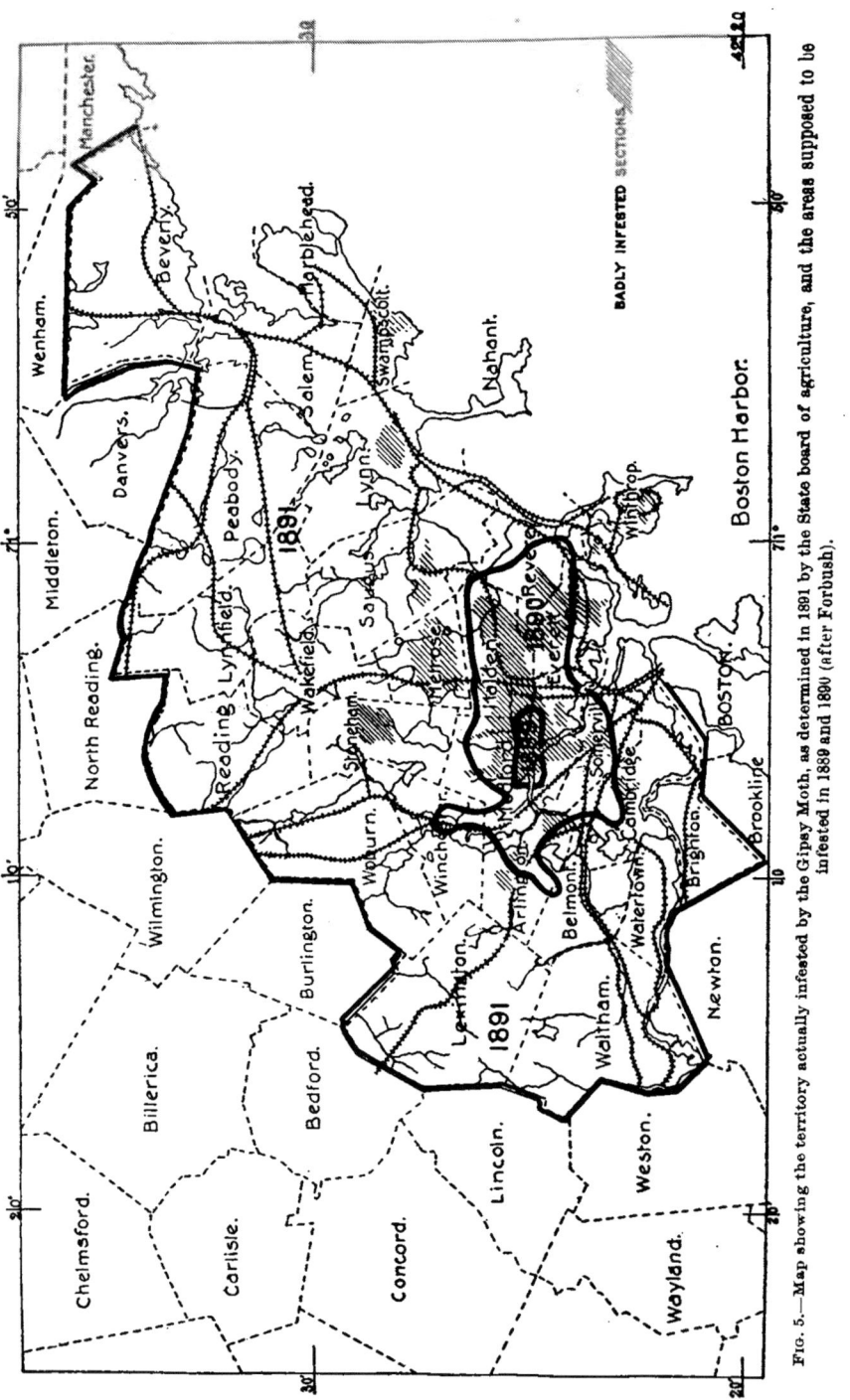

FIG. 5.—Map showing the territory actually infested by the Gipsy Moth, as determined in 1891 by the State board of agriculture, and the areas supposed to be infested in 1889 and 1890 (after Forbush).

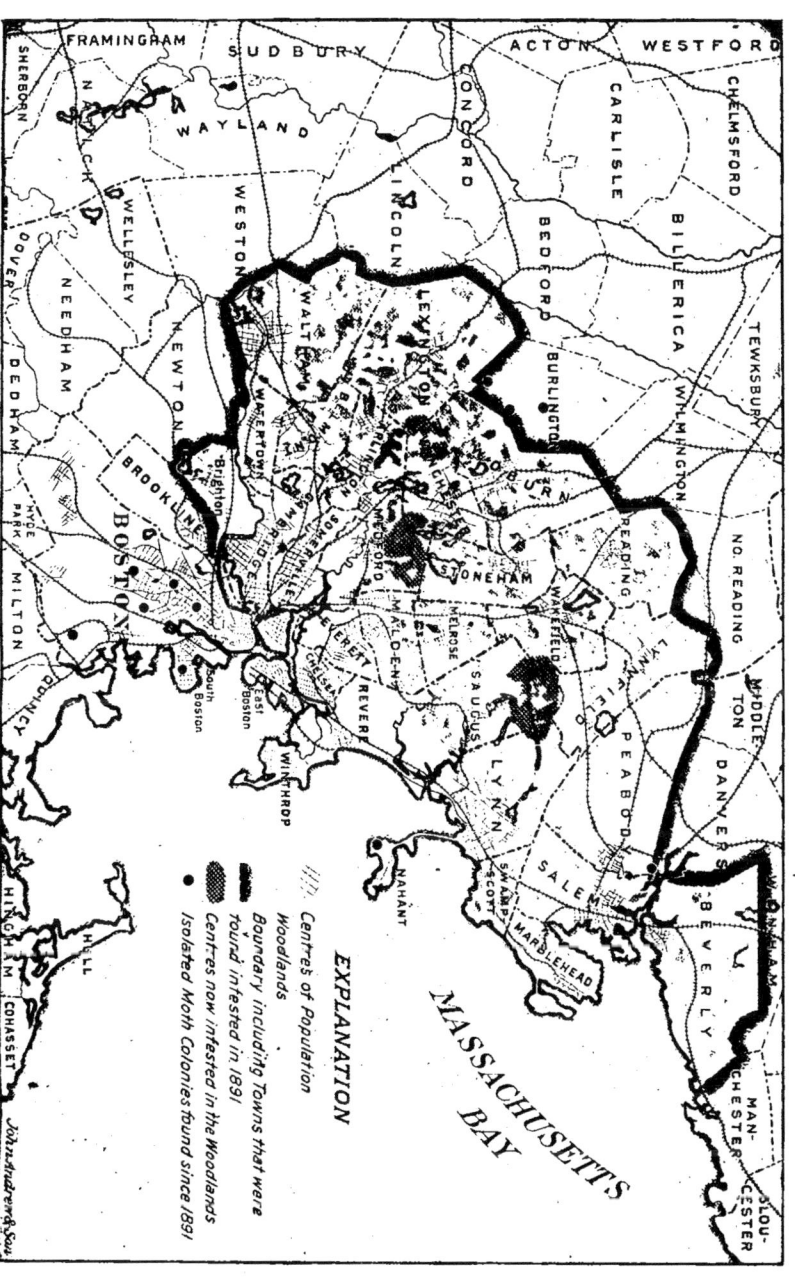

FIG. 6.—Map showing the region found infested in 1891, the colonies of the Gipsy Moth found since 1891 (but prior to 1896) outside that region, and the three principal centers of infestation and distribution in the woods (after Forbush).

therefore petitioned for an appropriation. Governor Brackett mentioned the outbreak in his message to the legislature, and as a result the joint committee of agriculture visited Medford and saw the masses of egg clusters on the trees. Finally an act appropriating $25,000 was passed. The act provided for the appointment of a commission of three persons to take charge of the work. Inspection work was at once undertaken to determine the extent of the region infested, and this inspection resulted in the establishment of the fact that the moth occurred over a much larger section of the country than had been supposed, and as a result an additional appropriation of $25,000 was made early in June.

In February, 1891, the first commission was removed by Governor Russell and a second one appointed. The first commission had been salaried and the second served without remuneration. This commission was superseded after a few weeks by the State Board of Agriculture, on their own recommendation, and in April an act was passed authorizing the board to carry into execution all reasonable measures to prevent the spread and secure the extermination of the insect. Unexpended appropriations were placed at the service of the board, and on June 30 an additional appropriation of $50,000 was made. A map of the infested region was the first work of the State board, and it was soon found that previous surveys had by no means indicated the complete distribution of the insect. In fact, the infested area, as it was supposed to have been determined in 1890, was at once enlarged by this new survey to at least five times its former size. The comparative estimates of 1889-90-91 are indicated on the accompanying map (fig 1). The survey of 1891 has been practically the basis of the work ever since that time, and it is interesting to note that, although a few colonies were soon after found in Danvers, Burlington, and South Boston, but three localities of infestation have since been found outside of the boundaries then laid down. These localities, in Brookline and Lincoln, will be mentioned in a later paragraph.

The organization of a competent field force was then begun and a detailed system of work was decided upon. Professor Fernald, of the Agricultural Experiment Station, was appointed entomological adviser to the subcommittee of the board in charge of the work. In January, 1892, the committee recommended an appropriation of $75,000 for the continuance of the work, and an act authorizing this appropriation was passed on March 1. An attempt was immediately made to destroy all egg clusters found on the roads in order to prevent the spread of caterpillars, and after the eggs had hatched, spraying operations were begun against the young caterpillars and the method of burlaping the trees was introduced against the larger larvæ. The appropriation was not sufficient to provide enough men to thoroughly examine the burlaps, yet during the summer the officers reported that nine-tenths of the insects in places known to be infested had been killed, and in many localities they had been exterminated. During the fall of this year an attempt was made to thoroughly search the country, but the lack of money was felt, and it was found necessary to discharge a large part of the force. In its annual report the committee requested an appropriation of $165,000 for the work in 1893. Instead of this sum, however, an appropriation of $100,000 was made on April 12, and fieldwork was at once begun. An increased force was put at work, and in general the same methods were adopted as had been used the previous year. At the close of this season an appropriation of $165,000 was again recommended to the legislature, and again the amount was reduced by the legislative body to $100,000, and this was not secured until May 23, when more than three weeks of the best working time of the season had been lost.

Full inspection this year revealed the presence of the insect in several localities not before known to be infested. This time an appropriation of $200,000 was asked for by the State board of agriculture. This proposition developed some opposition, and public hearings were held, and the legislative committee on agriculture finally resolved to call for an appropriation of $150,000, which was granted on May 17, 1895. Again valuable time had been lost, but work was immediately begun and carried through the season. In the winter of 1895-96 the board of agriculture recommended an appropriation of $200,000 for work during 1896, and also urged that the appropriation be promptly made in order to avoid the hindering of the spring work. An emergency appropriation of $10,000 was granted and became available April 28, but only $100,000 was granted for the work for the season of 1896, the remaining $90,000 becoming available June 4, too late, as the officials say, to carry out the plans made for the season's work, and necessitating a complete change in plans. Extra work was also made necessary by the hatching of the eggs which it had been planned to destroy in the spring had the appropriation been available at that time. The small amount of the appropriation would not admit of exterminative work over all of the infested territory, and in order to prevent the spread the outer towns were closely attended to through the season.

Two colonies were discovered this year in Brookline, just outside of the previously known infested territory. The discovery of these outside colonies, however, did not indicate any recent spread of the moth, as conclusive evidence existed that they had been established for a number of years, but had not been reported to the committee and had not been discovered by its inspectors.

In December, 1896, an appropriation of $200,000 was asked for work during 1897. On January 19, 1897, an advance of $8,333 was made, and a balance of $141,667 was made available February 26, making the appropriation for the year $150,000. The committee was thus enabled for the first time to begin work early in the season, and the results accomplished during the year 1897 have greatly exceeded in value those of any previous year.

METHODS USED BY THE STATE AUTHORITIES.

After the preliminary inspection work mentioned in the previous section had been largely accomplished, methods of actual destruction of the insect were adopted. In the course of the eight years during which this work has been carried on, there has been a steady improvement in the efficacy of the insecticide measures used. For a time these methods consisted almost entirely of the destruction of the egg masses, spraying with arsenical poisons for the caterpillars and killing the caterpillars under burlap bands on tree trunks, and these measures are to-day practically the only ones used where colonies exist in towns or on cultivated grounds. During the past two years, however, work has been carried on with great energy in forest lands, and here the means mentioned have been supplemented with extensive clearing out of underbrush, thinning out of the woods by the felling of a certain proportion of the timber, and by burning over the ground. When the writer first visited the infested region in the summer of 1894 the earlier methods only were in use. Nevertheless a number of original methods had been adopted, and he was impressed, as everyone has been who has thoroughly investigated the work of the State officials, with the systematic and thorough manner in which the remedial work was being carried on. He had nothing but praise for this work, and the only obstacle to the entire success of the effort which he foresaw was the occurrence of the insect in islands throughout large stretches of densely wooded country, where the methods then in use could hardly be completely effective. He did not anticipate the possibility of such radical woodland measures as have been instituted. But of this more will be said in a later paragraph.

The conspicuous color of the egg clusters and the long duration of the insect in this stage of existence, together with the fact that the destruction of an egg mass prevents much potential damage, very early suggested to the officials the feasibility and importance of fighting the insect in this stage. Indeed, one of the first measures adopted by the selectmen of Medford was the collection of egg clusters from the trunks of shade trees in the infested district. Moreover, it seems that this is the principal remedial measure adopted in Europe.

The great success, however, which had attended spraying operations against other leaf-feeding caterpillars in the United States caused certain economic entomologists to believe that the labor of collecting these egg clusters during the winter time was unnecessarily great, and that there would be much economy both in labor and money in waiting until the eggs hatched in the early summer and then spraying the surrounding vegetation with paris green or london purple. In fact, this argument was put forward very strongly by Professor Riley in his testimony before the State legislative committee on agriculture in Boston, March 4, 1891. It soon developed, however, that the Gipsy Moth caterpillar was unusually immune to the effects of arsenicals; that trees sprayed with the arsenicals, even if used at a strength sufficient to burn the foliage, would support these caterpillars without destroying more than a small proportion of them.

Efforts were therefore made to discover an arsenical compound which could be applied to trees at a strength considerably greater without burning the leaves. These efforts were successful, and the substance known as arsenate of lead was developed and is coming into general use, not only against the Gipsy Moth, but against other leaf-feeding insects. This substance may be sprayed upon the tenderest foliage at a dilution of 10 pounds to 100 gallons of water without injury, whereas 1 pound of paris green to 100 gallons of water frequently injures the leaves. Even with this valuable arsenical combination (the discovery of which, it must parenthetically be stated, has already proved of the greatest value to the economic entomologist) it was found that except under certain conditions spraying could not be generally adopted with perfect effect against the Gipsy Moth. A certain proportion of the caterpillars on sprayed trees always escaped, so that it can not be absolutely relied upon for exterminative work.

Moreover, extensive experimental work has shown that there is only about one month in the year during which effective spraying can be done. This is from about the 15th of May, when most of the caterpillars have hatched, to the 15th of June, when all have hatched, and when most of them have reached the age when they will cluster under the burlap. If, during this short period, there are two or three weeks of rainy weather, as is frequently the case, very little effective spraying can be done. Furthermore, a concentration of the work in this short season makes necessary a great expenditure for spraying apparatus, and necessitates the employment of a large force of men for this purpose—a difficult matter, since proper spraying requires expert hands.

The conditions under which spraying is still carried on and under which it is the only practicable remedy, are such as exist in certain parks—Franklin Park, for example, where there are extensive stretches of tangled vines and valuable shrubbery which hide the egg masses and which can not be banded, and which, at the same time, on account of their value, can not be burned over. Here spraying is still carried on, and with good effect, owing to repeated operations and great persistence, which, of course, involve a very considerable expense.

Different methods of egg destruction have been tried. The first recommended was to the effect that the eggs be scraped from the trees and burned. They were scraped off or cut away from the trunks on which they rested, placed in tin cans, and burned in stoves or brush fires. A fierce heat is required for their destruction. Whenever the eggs were very numerous in undergrowth or waste land, fire was run over the dead leaves and débris as an experiment, but this method seemed to have but little effect, as the heat was not sufficiently intense. The hairy cover seems remarkably nonconductive and renders the eggs impervious for a time to sudden heat. Some minutes are required to destroy them utterly. An ordinary brush fire merely scorched the outside layer and killed a few of the outside eggs. Next, experiments were made with crude petroleum, spraying it over the ground and igniting it, but this was not perfectly effective. Continued experiments were made with different methods. A remarkable apparatus was constructed to distribute inflammable oil in a spray which developed wonderful combustive powers. Many substances, both liquid and gas, were experimented with to destroy the eggs, and a series of interesting implements were invented in the way of hand mirrors to assist in searching for the eggs, and knives and scrapers for removing them and destroying them.

It resulted from this experimental work that creosote was found to be the best substance for egg destruction, and the present method consists in thoroughly painting each egg mass found with a cheap creosote oil. There are great difficulties in the way of economically and rapidly applying this remedy. The eggs must be searched for in inconceivable crevices, trees must be climbed and egg clusters, which can not be reached by hand, must still be painted by means of brushes attached to the extremities of long poles. The process, however, is carried on very effectively and much more rapidly than would be supposed. The men employed have become so trained in the discovery of eggs that they will see them instantly, even at the tops of tall trees, where they would be entirely unnoticed by nonexperts. A gang of men will proceed rapidly through a bit of woodland, treating the egg clusters in this way, and it is safe to say that after they have finished, and after the still keener eyed inspectors have followed up, the number of potential caterpillars has been reduced to a minimum.

After the eggs have hatched, the new method of work is at once introduced. According as conditions vary in different localities the director of fieldwork has varied his method of treatment. Thus, in the case of some colonies where the eggs were numerous, but concentrated within a comparatively small space, it has been considered advisable to allow them to hatch, and the work of destruction has in such cases been directed exclusively against the caterpillars. Where, however, the egg masses were more or less scattered, every effort has been made to prevent the appearance of the caterpillars by destroying the eggs. Against the caterpillars themselves several kinds of work have been carried on—the spraying previously mentioned and two methods of banding the trees. The first consists in placing around the trunk of the tree a viscid sticky band, either tar paper or fish oil, or the sticky German product known as "raupenleim" (caterpillar glue), applied directly to the bark. This substance, which has been used with good effect in Europe against the Gipsy Moth caterpillar and against the even more numerous and destructive larva of the nun moth, remains viscid for many months, and is very effective for the purpose for which it is used. The object of this sticky band is to prevent the ascent of the tree by young caterpillars hatching from egg masses at or near the surface of the ground. Extensive experiments and considerable practical work have been conducted with bands of this character in the course of the fight, but their use at present is not great, the officials concentrating their efforts in the main upon other means.

These sticky bands, however, are still used in one rather important connection. In forest work, where the eggs upon the trees have already been treated with creosote in the fall, the undergrowth cleared away, and the dead limbs burned, the colony is abandoned for the winter. Just before the time of the hatching of the caterpillars in the spring the sticky bands are placed around the trees and thus prevent the comparatively few caterpillars which may hatch from egg masses laid in hidden and undiscovered places at the surface of the ground, such as deep crevices between rocks, from ascending the trees. Thus, when all of the eggs have hatched, the remaining caterpillars can easily be destroyed by burning the ground over with a very ingenious and destructive apparatus, which has been invented in the course of the work, and which is known as the "cyclone burner."

The second band is used to entrap caterpillars which have already made their appearance in a given tree or the presence of which is suspected. After much experiment, the committee has adopted a simple strip of common burlap, which is tied about the tree with a single string at its middle, at about the height of a man's shoulders. The burlap is purchased in bales and cut into strips 12 inches wide. These strips are made into rolls, which the workmen carry suspended from the shoulder. Approaching the tree, the roll is passed around the trunk and enough cut off to encircle the tree and lap sufficiently at the ends to allow for shrinkage. A bit of twine is tied around both tree and cloth at the middle of the latter. The upper half of the burlap is then turned down over the twine, thus making a double band about the tree. The object of this banding is to assemble the caterpillars which may be upon the trees, since it has been found, as stated in an earlier sentence, that the larvæ feed at night and descend the trunk in search of hiding places during the day. Where the trunk and branches offer no better hiding places, most of the caterpillars will crawl down morning after morning and seek the shelter of the burlap. The men in making their rounds raise the burlap and cut or crush the caterpillars collected beneath it.

Many little details connected with the systematic examination of the burlap can not be touched upon, but it will suffice to say that the force at the disposal of the committee is so organized and the system of examination is so arranged that this method becomes a very effective and by no means so expensive a measure as might be supposed for destroying the caterpillars. Down to 1897 it was found that sooner or later practically all, in fact, I may almost say positively all, of the caterpillars in a given tree seek shelter under the burlap band except during very rainy weather. It will readily be seen that it is not at all necessary to examine the bands every morning, since the life of the caterpillar extends through several weeks, and examination at intervals of a number of days will thus suffice. So effective has this method of ridding the tree of the insect proved that one of the most experienced and efficient of the assistants in the work has told the writer that it is his firm opinion that the last Gipsy Moth larva in the State of Massachusetts will be caught under a burlap band.

Very much to the surprise of the workers, it was found that with the season of 1897 the caterpillars changed their habits to some extent, and that they sought the protection of the bands during the day with much less regularity than in previous years. It seems likely that this is to be accounted for by the fact that the breeding season of 1897 was an exceptionally dark and rainy one. The effort of the caterpillars in entering beneath the bands seems to have been for the purpose of avoiding the bright sunlight, so that when the sky was dark there no longer existed a necessity for this effort. The fact remained, however, that the bands were by no means as effective as they had been in previous years, and the workers were obliged to adopt a modification of the former methods. The extensive banding was done as usual in the spring, but the changed habit becoming apparent more spraying was carried on, and it was found that with the smaller trees a severe jar would cause most of the larvæ to fall to the ground, more or less suspended on their journey by silken threads. Upon reaching the ground they at once crawl actively to the base of the tree, where, entering the burlap band at a height of 4 or 5 feet, would creep under it, and were thus in condition to be destroyed by the next gang of men. This jarring method was adopted with great success in several bad colonies.

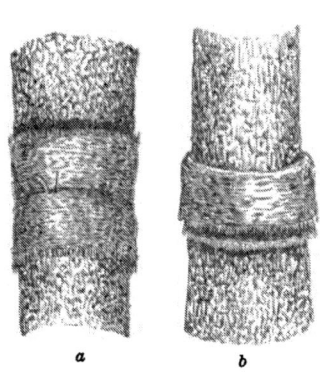

FIG. 7.—Manner of applying burlap bands: *a*, band as originally tied; *b*, band with upper half turned down—greatly reduced (after Forbush).

Toward the end of July, however, the weather changed radically. The long-continued spell of wet weather ceased and the caterpillars, to a certain extent, at least, resumed their normal habits and came to the bands; but by this time the examining of the bands had practically been discarded. They served a most excellent purpose, however, since in many localities perhaps the majority of the egg clusters were laid beneath them or in their immediate vicinity. Several badly infested regions were visited for example on the morning of November 17, in which it was noticed that almost every egg cluster on a given tree was to be found within a circle of a few inches from the band. This renders their treatment particularly easy, since the less expert men could be used for the work.

In the banding work it was soon found that the burlaps were most successfully used on well-kept trees with smooth, round trunks and branches. If the trees were originally in such condition or were first properly prepared, the insect was eradicated from many localities by the banding method alone, but when trees with decaying branches, hollow trunks, or rough or loose bark become infested the caterpillars frequently prefer the shelter afforded by such cavities or inequalities to that afforded by the burlap. As a result, the employees in placing the burlaps upon the trees throughout an infested region were obliged to prepare the tree in many cases. Dead branches were cut off, cavities were filled up or covered tightly with tin, and the rubbish and weeds were removed from the ground about the tree. This work was onerous and consumed much time, but it paid in the long run not only by bringing about the ready destruction of the worms under the burlap, but by greatly improving the health and appearance of the trees. The writer has seen many trees whose lives were undoubtedly saved by this sanitary treatment by the gipsy-moth workmen.

Experimental work was carried on sufficiently against the pupæ within their cocoons and against the moths to show that economic work against the insect in either of these stages could not be as successful as in other stages, although as a matter of fact thousands of the pupæ and moths are incidentally destroyed each year.

We have thus mentioned the main methods used against the insect in any one of its specific stages of life. Quite as important, however, has been the general work of the committee in the way of clearing up the breeding places and rendering the localities swarming with large colonies of the moth uninhabitable by them, or at least easy to treat successfully. Rubbish heaps have been cleaned up and neglected dooryards, pasture lots, and waste lands have been thoroughly renovated or burned over. The general work, however, which has been carried on in the woodlands has been still more arduous and important. Any one visiting certain places in the Middlesex Fells or in the Lynnwoods Park or any of the dense forest areas lying to the northeast of Boston, would be apt to say that an extermination of any species of insect in such jungles of vegetation would be impossible, and perhaps so it would were the Gipsy Moth scattered generally through this region, as seems to be the prevalent impression. Few people who have not visited the locality realize the character or extent of the woods in the outlying towns of Melrose, Lynnfield, Peabody, Medford, Stoneham, Wakefield, Saugus, Woburn, Winchester, and Lexington.

Although the country is very thickly settled—so much so that in driving along many of the roads one seems to be almost traversing a continuous village—yet standing upon some point of vantage like Castle Rock or Bear Hill, the whole country for miles around has almost the appearance of a virgin forest. The Gipsy Moth, however, is not generally distributed throughout this region, but occurs here and there—frequently at great intervals—in isolated and restricted spots, to which the workers have given the name colonies or groups of colonies. It is therefore unnecessary to work through hundreds of acres of woodland, but only here and there through patches of comparatively few acres. This distribution is readily accounted for by the fact that the insect spread from a common center in Medford, not by the flight of the moth, for the moth does not fly, but by caterpillars being carried upon the clothes of pedestrians, and upon buggies, market wagons, carts, and other vehicles, and crawling off again at some stopping place perhaps miles from the original center. This had been going on for years before the State work was begun.

Wherever circumstances favored the production of a female moth at one of these stopping places of the caterpillars and a male moth was at a near enough distance to allow it to fly to the female and fertilize her, there a colony was apt to be started the next year by the larvæ hatching from the consequent batch of eggs. Of course, many such additional colonies proved abortive and died out, but many others continued to propagate and to gradually spread, although very slowly. At the same time, however, when they had become of a certain size, they were again centers of distribution in the same way. Owing to the slowness of natural spread of the insect, very few of the colonies, so called, are of any great extent, so that by stamping out one here and one there and a third in some other place, a considerable extent of woodlands can be rid of the insect. Moreover, on account of the vastly less frequent traffic through woodland regions, the colonies are by no means as widespread and are in almost every case to be found in the immediate vicinity of the traversing roads.

In the case of these woodland colonies the committee at once realized that the work was very difficult and would have to be of the most thorough character, and in the carrying out of work of this thorough character, much opposition from the owners of the lands was anticipated. Such opposition has been found in some cases, while in others the committee has been agreeably surprised to find that the gravity of the case has brought about a disposition to permit almost any kind of exterminative work.

It is interesting to note that a large portion of the woodland which the committee has been obliged to treat was not owned by individuals, but belonged to the parking systems of the different towns. In a way this has facilitated the work of the committee, since they have been enabled to treat in such cases with one body for a large area; but in another way it has proved something of a hindrance, since the parking people have, in general, been less complaisant than individual owners.

Owing to the great desirability, and in fact the almost absolute necessity, of avoiding popular opposition, the committee has been loath to use the powers conferred upon it by law in the way of forcibly entering premises and carrying on the necessary work. It has much preferred to adopt the conciliatory measures of enlisting the owner's sympathy and support by showing the necessity of the work and reducing his loss to a minimum. The first measure which they have adopted in eradicating a woodland colony is to thin out the timber. This has been done in some places much more radically than in others. One extensive colony in the vicinity of Woburn it was thought could not be exterminated without the destruction of the entire timber growing upon a certain hill, and this was done.[1] In other cases about every third tree was cut down and its stump cut close to the ground; in still others, about half of the trees were thus felled, and in other cases only every third tree was left standing. In one exceptional case five-sixths of the trees were felled. The wood, as a measure of economy, was naturally saved in every case.

Practically no timber trees have been felled. Only very rarely has one been found which it has been necessary to cut. The poorer and smaller trees were invariably chosen, and these were cut up into cord wood and hauled away, and thus became a source of some recompense. After the thinning out, the underbrush was all cut down and the surface of the ground thoroughly burned over, the egg clusters upon the remaining trees being destroyed with creosote, and the trees themselves given a raupenleim band in the spring, burlaped where necessary, and watched through the ensuing seasons until satisfactory evidence was gained that the colony was exterminated. In many cases the actual value of the timber patch has been raised by the treatment given it by the gipsy moth people. The woods have simply been opened up to some extent, allowing more sun to enter and better growth on the part of the timber trees through the destruction of poorer soil-exhausting vegetation, while the sale of the firewood saved has been a profit to the owner of the land. In other cases, where the felling has been more extensive, the wood saved has been in the nature of a compensation rather than a profit. In certain cases, where owners remained obdurate, men with ready funds and more complaisant dispositions have been found who purchased the land and then permitted the work as a strict business venture. In still other cases, there was no ultimate intention of preserving the woods, and the clearing of the land by the committee has simply saved the owner the expense of doing it himself, and enabled him to carry out at once his plans of putting the land into cultivation or cutting it up into building lots.

---

[1] The exact steps taken in this operation were as follows: "The caterpillars appeared in the summer of 1895 in sufficient numbers to strip the leaves from the trees on two areas of an acre or more each, and it was found that they had scattered over some 15 acres in the immediate vicinity. All of the trees (largely oaks 40 to 60 feet in height) and the undergrowth of nearly 10 acres were burned, and the rest of the wood was cut and sold. The leaves were taken up and burned in the fall of 1895, and in the spring of 1896 the ground was all burned over. Although this burning left little on the land except stumps and ashes, a few caterpillars appeared later in the season around the edges and fed for a time on the sprouts which made their appearance after the fire. Here the ground was burned over again, and no traces of the insect have since been found."

By such work as this the caterpillar has already apparently disappeared in a number of these dangerous woodland colonies, and the employees of the committee claim that it has been exterminated.

A good idea of the activity of the committee and its employees may be gained from the following statement, showing the work done during the year 1896, and which is taken from the report of the State Board of Agriculture, published in January, 1897:

Work done during 1896.

Trees (fruit, shade, and forest):
- Inspected 10,718,836
- Found to be infested with caterpillars, pupæ, moths, or eggs 57,723
- In which cavities have been cemented or covered 3,408
- Burlaped 567,025
- Sprayed 4,327
- Trimmed 90,820
- Scraped 929
- Cut 132,391
- Acres of brush land and woodland cut and burned over 477

Buildings:
- Inspected 24,764
- Found to be infested 815

Wooden fences:
- Inspected 43,917
- Found to be infested 1,318

Stone walls:
- Inspected (rods) 18,997
- Found to be infested 633

Number of each form of the moth destroyed during the year by hand:
- Caterpillars 1,808,105
- Pupæ 441,899
- Moths 44,291
- Hatched or infertile egg clusters 31,501
- Unhatched and probably fertile egg clusters 884,928

OPPOSITION TO THE STATE WORK.

As has been indicated in a previous section, there has always been more or less opposition to the passage of acts before the legislature involving these large annual appropriations for the gipsy-moth work. On several occasions the committee on agriculture of the legislatures has listened to persons opposed to the work. The arguments brought forth by such individuals have in no case interrupted appropriations, but it is safe to suppose that some of the delays in making appropriations and some of the reductions in the amount from the estimates submitted by the State board of agriculture have resulted in part from this opposition. The writer has made an earnest effort to learn the grounds for this opposition. He has talked with a number of individuals, some of them scientific men of high standing, but has been unable to find a person holding opposing views who was sufficiently well informed about the work actually being done by the committee to thoroughly justify the expression of a positive opinion. In the main the opposition is based upon theoretical ideas, and a thorough acquaintance with what is actually being done renders these arguments void, with possibly one exception.

The writer was somewhat struck with the view expressed by one of these gentlemen in regard to the influence which the woodland work of the committee might have upon native birds. It was said that in the extensive partial deforestation and thorough clearing up of underbrush and burning over the dead leaves and low growth the nesting places of many birds were destroyed and the birds themselves were driven away. This seemed so important a matter that some attention was paid to it. It will be remembered that it has already been pointed out that none of this woodland work is general—that the insect occurs only in isolated colonies or in groups of colonies of slight extent compared with the forest area. A patch of a thousand acres of woodland, for example, may contain two or three infested localities, none of which will exceed 10 acres in extent, so that, admitting that the birds are temporarily driven from their nesting places in the areas worked over, they are not driven far and may shortly return to their original haunts. Moreover, the workers have this very matter distinctly in view, and they have even gone so far as to have constructed numbers of bird boxes, which are placed in appropriate situations for the purpose of attracting nesting birds.

Appreciating thoroughly as they do the aid that insectivorous birds afford them in their work, they endeavor to time, where possible, their operations in localities where birds abound in such a way as to interfere as little as possible with the nesting. The bird argument comes, too, from persons living in houses with old gardens, where the birds nest in the shrubbery. It becomes necessary sometimes to destroy this shrubbery in order to eradicate the moth, and, as a matter of course, the birds are here driven away temporarily. Moreover, the workers invariably break up, wherever possible, the nesting places of the English sparrow. So that after all the bird argument against the gipsy-moth work becomes unimportant.

THE INVESTIGATION OF THE WORK BY THE WRITER DURING 1897.

Although the writer was reasonably familiar with the conditions existing in the infested region and the results which had been accomplished, as well as the methods used by the committee and the means by which these results had been brought about, by virtue of two previous trips to Boston in the summers of 1894 and 1895, as well as from a familiarity with the published results of the work and from information gained by occasional meetings with the consulting entomologist and the director of the fieldwork at Washington, D. C., and during the summer meetings of the American Association for the Advancement of Science, he saw the absolute necessity for a careful investigation throughout an entire season before expressing such an opinion of the work as that called for by the Congressional act. In order, therefore, that no time should be wasted, work was begun immediately upon passage of the act, in April, although the legislation was not effective until the beginning of the fiscal year, July 1. At the latest possible moment before the bursting of the buds in the spring he visited Boston and watched carefully through several days the winter work of the committee in inspection, egg destruction, forest clearing, burning over of ground, and preparations for summer work, making at the same time a more or less careful round of the infested territory.

In May he again visited the headquarters of the committee in Malden, watched the work of this season, which consisted practically in burlaping trees in the portions of the territory in which this method was to be relied upon. In June the first assistant entomologist, Mr. Marlatt, who has for some years interested himself particularly in the matter of insecticides and insecticide appliances, was deputed to take up the work and carefully examine its progress and the general conditions and to formulate an independent opinion. In July the writer once more went over the ground, thoroughly investigating the critical midsummer work of the field force, and at the same time interviewed several persons who were opposed to the continuance of the State work on so large a scale. In September the expedition was repeated, the early fall work was looked into, and additional information gained. In November a final trip was taken for the purpose of verifying all doubtful points. At this time some of the most interesting and important work of the whole season in the way of the wholesale destruction of the egg clusters in the Medford woodland district about Pine Hill was being carried on. This work was studied, other portions of the regions were visited, and a number of persons were consulted.

PRESENT CONDITION OF THE INFESTED TERRITORY.

As the conclusions which we may justly draw from our summary of the work which the State of Massachusetts has done in this gipsy-moth investigation must be based largely upon the present condition of the territory in comparison with what its condition has been in previous years, we must be more detailed in this section of the bulletin than in others. It will be, in fact, impossible to present a satisfactory view of the present condition without detailed consideration of the exact facts connected with each of the thirty-two towns in the territory in question. These are given hereafter. It must be distinctly understood that while what is said under these headings of the condition of the different localities in the previous years has not all been substantiated by personal investigation on the part of the writer practically all of that which relates to conditions in 1897 has been so substantiated, and he is thoroughly convinced of the accuracy of the statements which follow.

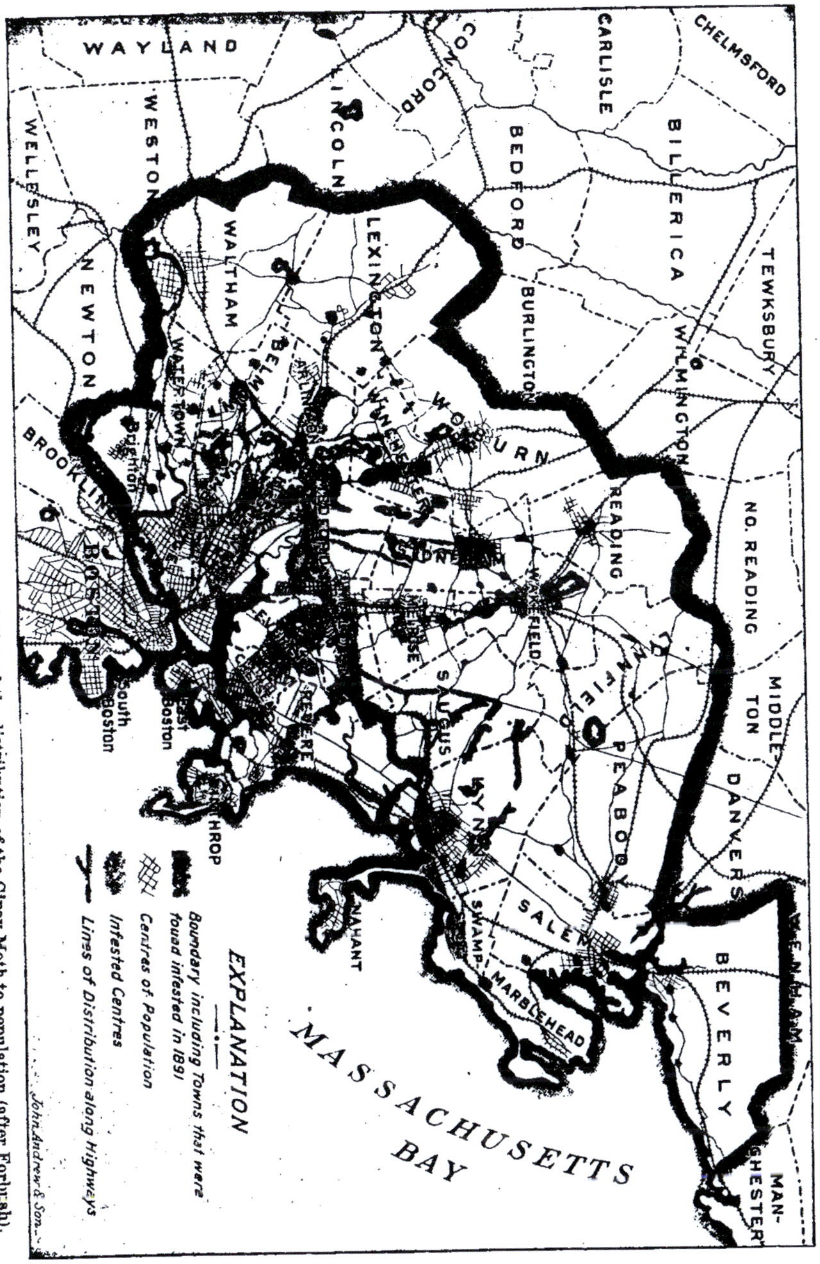

FIG. 8.—Map of the territory found infested in 1891, showing the relation of the distribution of the Gipsy Moth to population (after Forbush).

It must further be premised, in order that a distinct understanding of the statements may be had, that from the standpoint of a person unfamiliar with the conditions no portion of the infested territory contains at present many Gipsy Moths. The residential portions of the closely connected villages, where many colonies have existed in previous years and which at times in former years have been overrun with caterpillars, now contain almost none. Practically the whole of this residential portion (except Malden and Medford), including even the farming portion with its orchards, has been burlaped this season wherever the insect has been found within the last three years, and, in general, it is safe to say that only a few caterpillars have been found in any one locality. The workers have found it easy to distinguish between spots where an undiscovered egg cluster has been the previous winter and those where a straggling caterpillar or two have been brought in from more thickly infested woodland districts, as well as those where there have been only a few scattered eggs—no single sound egg cluster.

Where one or two egg clusters have hatched the present year, the colony is called a bad one in this residential district, so near to extermination has the work progressed! Practically, then, the insect can be found in numbers only in the woodlands. But from the fact that vehicles are constantly being driven through the territory every summer numerous caterpillars are conveyed from the woodlands into the villages, but are then almost invariably caught under the burlap bands. This scattering of caterpillars by carriages and carts has shown the committee, now that extermination is approaching and now that they have a good grasp on the entire territory, that the working policy must be altered to some extent. Instead of devoting a great majority of the funds to the outskirts it is necessary to at once reduce all colonies where the insects are present in number to what may be termed an "innocuous condition," since, so long as a single colony exists in which the insects are numerous, there will always be these stragglers, which may at any time start a new colony. How much depends upon this work may be illustrated by the fact that in the fall of 1897 a man was discovered carting leaves from one of the worst infested regions in the Medford woods into Somerville. A reinfestation of Somerville would probably have resulted. Experience has also shown that every summer at commencement time a few caterpillars are brought by visitors to the campus of Tufts College.

After this explanation the statements concerning the present condition of the infested towns will be perfectly understood.

ARLINGTON.

In the 1891 inspection this town was found to be badly infested, both in the woodlands and the open and cultivated lands. At present the territory east of Spy Pond is practically clear. Only two caterpillars were found there last year. In the woodland districts only two colonies of any extent exist at the present time. In the western part of the town an occasional egg cluster has been found this year. Nothing has been done in the town for two years except burlaping, and this year in taking off the burlaps all egg clusters found were destroyed. In spite of this paucity of work the town is in better condition than it was two years ago, and with means the extermination of the insect from the whole town is only a question of a short time.

BELMONT.

This was one of the towns early found infested (1890), and the later inspection showed the insect along the roads, on the farms, and also in the woods. Many of the colonies were exterminated prior to 1896, and during the present year much good work has been done there. Only an occasional caterpillar can now be found. The residential portion of the town was burlaped and the insects which now occur there are in the shrubbery about residences where the people have objected to the work.

BEVERLY.

In this town the insect was practically exterminated in 1896. In 1897 old localities have been inspected once or twice, but nothing has been found. The original colonies, of which there were about ten, have been wiped out of existence.

BOSTON.

Prior to 1896 the insect was practically exterminated in East and South Boston. One colony in South Boston was cleared in 1896 and in 1897 several dozen caterpillars were taken under burlap. These had evidently been brought in on vehicles. The Dorchester district was badly infested several years ago, but in 1897 only an occasional caterpillar was found, and no egg clusters were found on careful inspection in the fall. In the Roxbury district, which was considerably infested in 1894, nothing was found on careful inspection this year. Franklin Park, which has been referred to in a previous section, and which contained in 1893 an old colony which, owing to conditions, was very difficult to exterminate, has been absolutely free of caterpillars both in 1896 and 1897. In Brighton and Charlestown the insect appears to be exterminated. All the old colonies were burlaped and inspected in Brighton and but one caterpillar was found. This had evidently been brought in accidentally from some other portion of the territory.

BROOKLINE.

Two important colonies of the moth were found in Brookline in 1896. This town is outside of the infested territory as mapped in 1891. These colonies were of several years' growth, and the most energetic work was done in 1896 and 1897. A thorough inspection of the town was made in the winter of 1896–97 and no other colonies were found. The adjoining portions of the town of Newton were also inspected for a distance of 2 miles, and nothing was found. The work in both colonies has been thorough. In the immediate vicinity all trees have been carefully burlaped. About 20 egg clusters, however, were found at the extremity of the colony on the Schlesinger estate, which shows that further work will have to be done next year. The other colony, that upon the Crafts' estate, was so thoroughly worked over during the winter of 1896-97 that apparently but two egg clusters escaped. One of these was under a building and the other under a stone covered with snow. The caterpillars hatching from these two egg clusters were probably all trapped by burlap.

BURLINGTON.

A woodland colony discovered in 1895 furnished the only caterpillars which occurred in any numbers in 1896. This colony was thoroughly worked over in the winter of 1896-97, and during the present season a few caterpillars were caught by the bands, but no egg clusters were laid, so far as could be found. Traffic through the northern part of the town necessitates a tree-to-tree inspection, which will be given it next summer.

CAMBRIDGE.

The town of Cambridge has been comparatively neglected until the present season. Nearly every tree in the town was burlaped in 1897 and a few caterpillars were found. In many old localities of importance none at all were found. Only here and there were enough caterpillars found to indicate the occurrence of a complete egg cluster. In North Cambridge, which has been the worst section, only three caterpillars were found, evidently stragglers from some other locality. The portion of the town west of Harvard Square and Massachusetts avenue is now the worst infested region. There were three or four places where quite a number of caterpillars were found, but the probabilities are that all were captured. In Mount Auburn Cemetery, formerly a very badly infested district, very few caterpillars remain.

CHELSEA.

A few egg clusters were found in Chelsea in 1896, whereas the insect was generally scattered about the city in 1891. Most of the colonies were exterminated prior to 1896. Burlaping in the most suspected localities was resorted to in 1897 and a very few larvæ were found, although more may be brought in owing to the constant traffic with Everett and Malden.

DANVERS.

The two colonies previously known in Danvers were reported as having been exterminated in 1896. The town, however, has not been carefully inspected for two years and stragglers may have been brought in. It needs a new inspection.

EVERETT.

This town was badly infested in 1891, but was in fair condition in 1894. Comparatively little work was done in 1895, owing to pressure elsewhere, and the insect increased. During 1896 the town was burlaped and inspected. More caterpillars were taken there in 1896 than in any other city or town. It 1897 it was rather generally burlaped, and several thousand caterpillars were taken. A few egg clusters were found at the end of the season, which indicates a necessity for careful burlaping again in 1898.

LEXINGTON.

In 1896 it was reported that the greater portion of Lexington was cleared. In two colonies in the woodland in the northern portion of the town much work was done during the winter of 1896-97. During the summer of 1897 nothing was taken under burlaps in one of these colonies, showing the insect to have been exterminated. In the other a few caterpillars were found, but no egg clusters, indicating that extermination was probable also in this colony. In East Lexington village a few caterpillars were found in 1896. In 1897 there was no evidence of any hatching, and only an occasional caterpillar was taken, which had evidently been brought in on some vehicle. The eastern corner of the town extends into one of the badly infested spots in the woodland, and many trees were found infested in some of the woodland colonies in 1896. Much work was done there in the winter and spring. There was a woodland fire in the spring at one point, and only a few caterpillars were found under burlap in the summer. A number of egg clusters were found this fall. Work in these woods was not carried on very extensively, for the reason that the owner intends to cut off the timber. All of the old orchard and village colonies in this town are extinct.

LINCOLN.

A new colony was found in Lincoln during 1897. This is well outside of the territory mapped in 1891. It was reported to the State board by persons who noticed the stripped trees and who sent in caterpillars in July. Some trees were entirely covered. The colony was certainly several years old. A force of men was set at work immediately. About 4 acres of ground was cut over and about 6 acres burned over, and in the center of the colony the number of insects was reduced about 90 per cent. Apparently the insect is distributed more or less sparsely over about 100 acres of difficult ground to work over, since it contains many stone walls and loose ledges of rock. Next spring all of the small brush will be burned when the larvæ are small and the stone walls will be burned over in May, which will kill at least two-thirds of the larvæ. New sprouts will then come out, thus concentrating the remaining larvæ, and a new burning in July will kill most of these larvæ.

LYNNFIELD.

In all the colonies in Lynnfield known before 1894 the moths were exterminated in that year or previously. Further inspection in 1895 showed several colonies in the woodland. Some of these were extensions of Saugus colonies and others had existed in the woodland for several years. By the close of 1896 these woodland colonies had been nearly exterminated, the brush having been cut down and burned and the trees burlaped for two years. No insects were found in some of them in 1896, while in others a few were found. In the spring of 1897 a thorough search for egg clusters was made and a few eggs were found. All the colonies were burlaped and a very few larvæ were found, indicating the presence of scattered eggs, but of no complete egg clusters. The territory in November, 1897, was being inspected for egg clusters. None had been found up to the date of writing. A search of part of the woodland in the town was made in 1896, which showed only one small new colony. Owing to the extent of the woodland in this town and its popularity as a place for outings and picnics, the attention of the workers has been concentrated upon it.

LYNN.

At one time over twelve hundred estates in Lynn were infested, mostly in and about the center of population. In 1896, during the fall inspection, egg clusters were found in only one estate out of the 1,200. This was in a bad colony found in 1895. In the fall of 1895, 2,000 egg clusters were found in this colony. As a result of the remedial treatment, however, in the fall of 1896, only one egg cluster could be found. In 1897, as a result of burlaping, only one larva was found and that was on the outskirts of the country and had evidently been brought in on some vehicle. The extensive and beautiful "Lynn Woods Park" is in this town, and the Gipsy Moth obtained a foothold in these woods several years ago. During June, 1896, a colony was found in these woods, where the caterpillars had become so numerous as to strip the leaves from the trees and all vegetation over a small area. In the spring of 1897 inspection was carried on in these woods down to the time of the hatching of the caterpillars, and all known infested places were treated and the trees burlaped. In 1896, 107,520 caterpillars, 41,535 pupæ, and 11,027 egg clusters were taken in the park colony referred to, and in 1897 the number was reduced to 29,088 larvæ and 926 pupæ. The territory has not been as yet inspected for eggs, but it will be gone over if possible in the spring of 1898. There is not the slightest danger now of serious injury to the park, and the entire woods can be freed from the moth in a comparatively short time.

MALDEN.

This town, although badly infested in the early nineties, has not been injured of late, except in a few cases. During 1896 there was an outbreak in the southern part of the city where the trees on about half an acre were more or less defoliated. About half of the trees were cut down and the undergrowth cleared out. Nearly the whole town has been gone over and the eggs destroyed this fall. The proximity of the town to the Middlesex Fells renders the occurrence of straggling caterpillars more or less frequent, and the condition of the town at the close of the season of 1897 was certainly no better than at the close of 1896.

MARBLEHEAD.

In the fall of 1896 one small colony was found in the southeastern portion of the town, near Swampscott, and two egg clusters were found near the center of the town, although in previous years about a dozen colonies have been known in different portions of the town. In the southeastern colony all of the egg masses which could be found were destroyed and the trees cleaned up. It was in tillage land, partly in orchard, with willows growing along a stone wall. The trees were banded with insect lime in the spring of 1897, and after the larvæ were hatched the wall and low vegetation were burned over. Burlap bands were placed on the trees, and outside of the burned portion 126 caterpillars were found during the summer. None were found on the burned portion. Outside of the burlap limits two egg clusters were found, In the center of the town, where the two egg clusters were found in the fall of 1896, not a single caterpillar was taken.

MEDFORD.

This is the town in which the insect was originally found, and has contained as many as a hundred colonies in previous years. At the present time, outside of the Medford Woods, there are not more than three or four spots where they are present in any numbers. The central and southern part of the Medford Woods may be said to be rather badly infested and the colonies almost continuous. In the eastern and western sections there are by no means as many. In the northern portion, near Stoneham, there are only very small and scattered colonies. The whole woods will be thoroughly inspected if the means will allow. In November, 1897, the worst colonies were in process of treatment. The woods were being thinned out and the egg clusters destroyed with creosote. The whole place has been reported in good condition for exterminative work next season. A number of the worst colonies have already been cleared.

MELROSE.

In 1896 it was reported that a large amount of work remained to be done in the southern portion of the town, especially in the woodlands. This town was well inspected last winter, and in the whole northern portion only one colony was found in which the insects occurred in any number. Some of the oldest and worst colonies seem to be wiped out.

The Cedar Park colony (a very bad one) is evidently exterminated. There still remains, however, a wooded section which should have a tree to tree inspection.

NAHANT.

Four colonies have been known at Nahant, but all have been exterminated. There is so much travel to this delightful summer resort, however, that stragglers are likely to be brought in at any time.

NEWTON.

A single male pupa was found in the town of Newton in September, 1897. The nearest infested area is in Watertown, a mile and a half away. Some banding will be done about the spot where this pupa was found next season, but it is not likely that any caterpillars will be caught. A single tree in the Crafts' colony in Brookline is situated over the Newton border. The condition of this colony was described under Brookline.

PEABODY.

Down to 1896 all of the colonies in this town except three had been exterminated. One of these was reported in the fall of 1896 to be a large woodland colony which it would take some time to exterminate. These three colonies are known as the Newhall, the Marsh, and the Spring Pond colonies. The Newhall colony is near the Lynnfield line. It was burlaped in 1897 and two caterpillars found. No egg clusters were found after close examination in the fall. This colony, therefore, is probably exterminated. The Marsh colony is on Summit street, in the West Peabody woods. In the spring of 1897 two egg clusters were found. Ten thousand trees were burlaped, and in the entire summer only one caterpillar was found, which, therefore, was evidently a straggler. No eggs could be found in the fall, when the colony was carefully inspected. It is safe to say that this colony was also exterminated, and that it is not worth while to burlap another season. The Spring Pond colony is the woodland one referred to in the opening sentence. Here 130,000 larvæ were taken in 1896. In January the territory was gone over for eggs, and but two egg clusters were found. In 1897 the whole territory was carefully burlaped, and 400 larvæ taken in two spots. Inspection in the fall of 1897 showed no eggs. In the summer of 1897 a yard in the center of the village was found to be infested. The colony was probably 2 years old, and the insect was accidentally introduced by the owner. Thorough work in this colony has reduced it to insignificant proportions.

READING.

This town has been considered free for the past two years. Inspection, however, this season shows that stragglers have been introduced and that there must have been scattered eggs the past winter, a thing which is not likely to occur again.

REVERE.

Only one egg cluster was found in the residential portion of this town in 1896, whereas they occurred in all parts of the town in 1891. On account of the constant traffic through the town an occasional caterpillar has been found during the past season. In the woods near the Saugus and Malden lines a number of caterpillars were caught under burlaps the present season.

SALEM.

Nearly all of the colonies that were found near the center of population in this town, and there were many, were exterminated by 1896. The very bad colony at Harmony Grove Cemetery is certainly exterminated. The region known as the Salem Great Pastures, containing thick brush, was generally infested, and all the work that was feasible with the means provided was done up to 1896. It was then reported that in many cases the work had been a success and in others the lack of money resulted in cessation of work and consequent failure to exterminate. This year all known colonies in the pastures were gone over, beginning in April. The brush was cut and burned and wherever larvæ or eggs were found the region was burned over with oil. The trees were trimmed and burlaped and the whole region is now in excellent condition. It is possible that an occasional egg cluster will be left, but no inspection can be made this fall.

SAUGUS.

This is one of the worst towns. Colonies were found in the woodlands in 1893 and 1894, some of them quite large. The insects were held partially in check, but in 1896 they were reported to have increased and extended their limits, threatening not only to extend still farther into Saugus woods, but to reinfest Lynn, Salem, Swampscott, as well as other places where the moth was then nearly exterminated. In the winter of 1896-97 and in the spring of 1897 egg clusters were treated in these woods in all known colonies. Throughout these same colonies about 150,000 of the smaller trees were cut out, as well as the underbrush. The remaining trees were then burlaped and carefully watched during the summer. The effect of this careful work is well indicated by the following example: In what is known as Colony 17 during the fall and winter of 1896-97, 76,000 egg clusters were taken. In the same colony under burlaps during the summer 130,000 caterpillars were taken, and in the fall of 1897 rigid inspection showed six egg clusters only. This was a very difficult block of woods to work in, containing high pine trees, in which the moths as a general thing laid their eggs at a considerable elevation above ground. In the other colonies the work has resulted in about the same way. All of these spots will be burlaped next year. The egg inspection during the fall of 1897 occupied only about one-fourth of the time given to it the previous winter. The villages of Saugus were not burlaped during 1897, and there are probably a few egg clusters here and there. They will be inspected this fall or winter. It is likely that other colonies will be found in the Saugus woods, but this season's experience has shown how thoroughly they can be worked another year.

SOMERVILLE.

The insect in 1891 was scattered in colonies throughout the greater portion of this town. A steady improvement in the condition of the city was noted down to 1896, in which year all of the known colonies were carefully attended to. The present season almost nothing has been found in this town, but straggling caterpillars are constantly being brought from the Medford line. Two small colonies resulting from this fact have been found this fall. They are only in spots where an occasional egg cluster has not been found on account of the inaccessibility of its situation.

STONEHAM.

The whole town was partially burlaped in the summer of 1897 and scattered caterpillars were found which had probably been brought in from the Middlesex Fells. The fells colonies in this town have been watched and burlaped and have greatly improved, especially in the southwestern corner. Very few caterpillars were taken except at the Medford line, where they had been brought over from the Medford woods. In the northern portion of the town only an occasional caterpillar has been found.

SWAMPSCOTT.

The insect swarmed in certain parts of this town in 1891. The largest colony and one of the worst in the whole infested region was early cleared, and no trace of the insect can now be found there. This colony covered about 100 acres, a large part of which was woodland. At the close of 1896 it was reported that there was a small colony in the woodland of Swampscott and three localities in which the egg clusters were found. The three colonies where eggs were found during 1897 were burlaped, but only enough larvæ taken to indicate scattered eggs; not even the occurrence of a single whole egg cluster. No egg clusters were found in the fall of 1897, although close inspection has been made. The small woodland colony was cut over in the spring and then burlaped, but so few larvæ were found that it did not require burning. None were found in the center of the colony, but on the outside a very few, indicating that perhaps two or three egg clusters in rocks had escaped attention.

WAKEFIELD.

Although the insect was numerous in this town in 1891-92, its condition was improved by work to such an extent that at the close of 1896 only five colonies were found, and few insects were found during that season. The present season it is safe to say that all the upper region of the town is free from the insect. A few scattered larvæ seem to have been brought in from the Saugus woods, but all of the old colonies are practically extinct.

WALTHAM.

All of the old colonies in this town were practically exterminated previous to 1895. In 1896 one colony was found in the woods, which was carefully watched, burlaped, and treated in such a way as to promise extermination. Examination of this colony in 1897 shows that this work was effective. A single white-oak tree at the border of the colony, however, probably harbored a single egg cluster, as a few caterpillars were captured. Probably no more work will be required in this town, although the locality just mentioned will be carefully watched another season, and eventually another tree to tree inspection will be made. As Waltham is one of the border towns, this result is most encouraging.

WATERTOWN.

Although this town contained numerous colonies, all but two had been exterminated by the close of 1896. The 1897 inspection showed that in one of these the insect had been exterminated. The other is an extension of Mount Auburn Cemetery, in Cambridge, which has already been mentioned under the head of Cambridge. Very few caterpillars were found there this summer.

WINCHESTER.

The Winchester woodland contained a part of one of the badly infested wooded localities reported upon in 1895. Careful work was done in 1896 in the western Winchester woods. It was followed up by careful winter work. Considerable tracts were cut over and burned over, then inspected and burned again. The numbers of the insect were very greatly reduced and very few individuals can now be found there. In one of the worst colonies 33 acres of woodland was cut over by the owners and the brush burned off by the committee and the ground and sprouts burned over. No evidence of the insect has since been found in this tract of land, except at two points on the outskirts, where the wood was not cut and where a few caterpillars have been trapped this summer. In another colony the committee cut off the wood from about 10 acres and this wood was marketed by the owner of the land. In the southeastern borders of the town is a tract of farming land where there have been strips of badly infested woodland. Much of this was cut and cleared up in the spring of 1897 and vast numbers of eggs destroyed by fire. This work and this summer's burlaping has so greatly reduced the insect as not only to prevent its spread, but to promise practical extermination almost in a single season. In the residential portion of the town the condition is excellent and only occasional caterpillars are found.

WINTHROP.

This town, although generally infested at one time, was carefully inspected in the fall of 1896 with the result that only three small egg clusters were found. A few caterpillars were trapped in the summer of 1897, but no egg clusters were found in the fall, so that the town is free from the insect except for stragglers which may appear in another year, and it must be remembered that the possibility of bringing in stragglers another year will be very greatly less than last season, owing to the radical work which has been done in the woodland colonies.

WOBURN.

The village and southern portions of the town of Woburn have been rather badly infested, but in 1896 it was reported that no moths were known to exist in the town at that time, except in the southwestern portion, near the Winchester-Lexington boundary. In 1897 there were only two places in which any number of caterpillars were found. Both were in old stone walls covered with vines. These localities were thoroughly burned out. In the southwestern woods a considerable number of caterpillars were captured near the place where old colonies had been destroyed the previous winter, but extermination in these dangerous places has nearly been reached. Were there no reinfestations from the neighboring borders of Winchester and Lexington, there would be no difficulty in absolutely clearing the town of Woburn in a very short time with sufficient means.

THE TERRITORY AS A WHOLE.

The infested territory as a whole now includes portions of 33 towns, portions of 31 towns having been included in the line drawn after the inspection of 1891. There have been at one time or another since 1891 within this territory, which, by the way, comprises approximately 220 square miles, 1,893 so-called colonies of the insect, a colony meaning a circumscribed spot infested by caterpillars. A colony may be very small and contain comparatively few insects, or it may cover a space of a number of acres and contain caterpillars by the thousand. At the present time it is safe to say that more than nine-tenths of these 1,893 colonies have been practically exterminated. The 1891 boundary line of the infested territory could at the present time be drawn in to a very considerable extent, although, at present, there exist the remains of three colonies outside of that boundary line, viz, two in Brookline and one in Lincoln. Throughout the residential and cultivated portions of the territory, as a whole, the Gipsy Moth is a scarce insect. The dangerous colonies which still exist are in the woodlands, and at present every one of these is in such condition that the insect is well in check. The consequence of the prompt availability of the funds appropriated by the legislature of 1896–97 has been that the entire field is well in view and that the prospects are more encouraging than ever before.

CONCLUSIONS.

It results from this reasonably thorough investigation that the writer is in position to say, as preliminary to his conclusions concerning future work, that the State of Massachusetts is most heartily to be congratulated upon the manner in which this work has been carried on. The effort of the State will rank as one of the great experiments in economic entomology in the history of the world. On the whole, it can be safely said that there has been no waste of the State funds. The officials in charge had to feel their way at first, but, contrary to the history of novel enterprises of this kind, there have been no disastrous experiments. The work has been admirably directed toward the main end almost from its inception. No criticism can be made, even in the light of present experience, of any of the work carried on since it has been in the hands of the State board of agriculture. The methods used have been not only sensible but ingenious to a high degree. No promising line of experiment has been neglected, and many have been followed out which would not have suggested themselves to less able and original minds than those having charge of the work. Results have incidentally developed which have already had a much wider and more important bearing than the destruction of this one insect, and it is safe to say that, even at this time, the total outcome of the work has been of great value, not only to the country at large but to all civilized portions of the globe.

The organization of the corps of workers, the selection of the men, the systems, not only of supervision, but of general organization, down to the simplest details and the economical expenditure of the funds, all seem as nearly perfect as can be desired. The writer has talked at length with all of the principal men connected with the work, has studied unnoticed the operations of the gangs of men in the field, has earnestly endeavored in every possible way to substantiate critical comments which have come to his ears, and is honestly convinced of the truth of all of his statements, which he nevertheless realizes may seem at first reading to be overenthusiastic. The most interesting feature of the investigation and one which is rarely seen in such State work is the vivid interest taken by practically all of the employees in the thoroughness and success of the work. The principal men are full of enthusiasm, full of the importance of their labors to the interests of the State, and at the same time full of a genuine and vivid scientific interest in the great experiment which they are helping to carry on. So great has been the interest and so arduously have they labored that in several cases they have broken down in health. The field director of the work was seriously ill through many weeks of the present season, one of the superintendents of sections has lost his health entirely from overwork, and another I have seen dragging himself about in the field superintending his men when he ought to have been in bed.

It follows then that the work which has been done has been wisely done and has been economically done. When we say that it has been wisely done, we mean that, admitting that the State fight is or was to be for the extermination of the species, the steps taken have been wise ones, and after a review of the entire work, and after the consideration of what is known as the habits of the insect, as well as of local conditions in 1889, it can not but be admitted that the effort of the State to exterminate the insect has also been wise. It is true that a large amount of money has been expended, and it is also true that much more money must be expended before extermination can be accomplished; but it is undoubtedly safe to say that the money which has been and will be spent by the State in this work is but as a drop in the bucket to the loss which would have been occasioned by the insect had it been allowed to spread unchecked. This loss would have fallen not only upon the State of Massachusetts, but upon other States of the Union, so that we may say that the State work has not only been wisely done, but that it has been patriotically done. At the present time there can be little doubt that the extermination of the insect is possible and that it will be only a question of a few years, if adequate State appropriations are continued. The simple fact that it has unquestionably been exterminated over considerable stretches of territory and that extensive colonies existing in the most disadvantageous territory for the prosecution of remedial work have been so thoroughly destroyed that not an individual has been found for three years with the most rigid annual inspection is sufficient proof of this possibility, for what can be done for one section like this can be done for all, if the means be sufficient.

Thus the questions as to whether the State has done the right thing in appropriating for the extermination of the insect instead of for holding it in subjection, and as to whether the money has been used in the best possible way to forward this end, may both be answered emphatically in the affirmative. The condition of the infested territory at the time of writing (November, 1897) is by far better than it has ever been before. This fact is largely owing to the promptly available appropriations of January and February, 1897. A great amount of admirably effective work was done at the critical time of the year, and the results are obvious. The writer believes that the condition of the entire infested territory at the present day is such that with the prompt appropriation of the amount asked for by the committee at the beginning of the coming session of the legislature the work which will be carried on during 1898 will be of so effective a character that even those who most gravely doubt the policy of the State efforts will be convinced of the efficacy of the work. A continuation of the appropriations for a few more years is unquestionably a necessity. Were the appropriation to lapse a single year, the work which has been done during the past six years would largely be lost. The $775,000 already appropriated would have been spent in vain.

There is one rather serious point which still remains to be considered. It has been shown that three large colonies of the insect have been discovered during the past two years outside of the boundaries of the survey of 1891. If such colonies—all of them of at least four years' standing and one of them of at least eight years' standing—have only just been found, may there not be others the existence of which is still unsuspected by the committee? It is probable that this is the case, and it seems to the writer that not only should a warning circular be sent to almost every property holder in a border of at least two towns deep around the line of 1891 with a request to inform the committee of the existence of caterpillars which resemble that of the Gipsy Moth, but that a thorough inspection of these same towns with as large a force as can be devoted to the purpose should be made in the near future. The knowledge of the Gipsy Moth work is now so widespread in Massachusetts and people have become so much interested in the work that it is not likely that many such colonies will be found, yet knowledge as to the existence of every one is an immediate necessity.

Printed by Libri Plureos GmbH in Hamburg, Germany